Thank you to my parents
Elvis M. & Margie D. Coleman
God Bless their cooking souls

This book is dedicated to my children; Trey and Kira, I love you with all my heart.

SOUL FOOD 101

Soul food, like jazz is improvisational. You develop a feel for it and everyone has their own style. The recipes in this book are my own culinary interpretations of common selections. Versions of these recipes have been passed down to me from my parents who were amazing cooks born and raised in Mississippi. Your families may add a different twist, go with it, its jazz, there are really no rules.

My palette is eclectic so I have also imported dishes from other cultures and interpreted them through a soul food veil. Remember, Soul food comes from the heart and the most important ingredient is love.

I am not a nutritionist, even though I have interpreted classic dishes with a healthier twist. That being said, while I don't use salt pork, I do use salt. While I may use olive oil, I also use butter (but much less than my ancestors) and I only use real sugar, no substitutes. The most important rule of soul food is –IT MUST TASTE GOOD! Otherwise, what's the point?

I am a lover of food who endeavors to live a long healthy life. I do indulge and therefore I work out, religiously, and I hope you will to. After all, the longer you live, the more you get to eat!

Soul Food terminology is different. Soul Food sauté is lightly tossing food in a little bit of light oil over medium heat. We know that the definition defines it as cooking at high heat in a wok until you hear it sizzle but that definition does not apply to soul food.

We also know that by definition a cobbler does not have a top crust. But by divine order, **soul food cobblers do** so get over it and don't waste your time writing me any emails trying to correct what will never change.

You will find other terms you don't agree with, ingredients you would not use or variations on these recipes that your mama didn't do. That's all good. Refine the recipes to fit your family's taste buds and health needs, and traditions.

For **video demonstrations** and more recipes, please visit my website at www.thejoyofsoulfood.com . Sign up and continue to receive helpful cooking tips. I have tried to keep the recipes as simple as possible with easy step by step instructions. Over the years I have filmed myself creating many dishes for you as well, check them out at the site, www.thejoyofsoulfood.com

Shopping List
Soul Food cooking uses some basic ingredients, please make sure to have these on hand to avoid frustration:
- Lawry's Seasoned Salt
- Black Pepper
- Salt
- Vegetable Oil
- Olive Oil
- Vinegar
- Sugar
- Butter
- Onions
- Garlic Powder
- Onion Powder

It's good to have the following equipment:
- 10" Cast Iron Skillet for frying and for cornbread and 10 " tube pan,
- Bundt cake pan
- Three 8 or 9 inch cake pans for cakes.
- large heavy bottom stock pot for greens, gumbo and low country boils

Now, let's go!
-Pamela Holmes

Table of Contents

Breads

For sopping gravy, jam, etc

Corn Bread

6 T vegetable oil
2 cups Corn Meal Mix
5 T sugar
1½ cups milk
2 eggs

1. Heat oven to 350 F.
2. Heat vegetable oil in 10-inch cast iron skillet or rectangular baking pan in oven 3-5 minutes
3. In large bowl combine all remaining ingredients and mix well.
4. Remove hot skillet from oven and tilt to coat pan evenly.
5. Pour excess oil into the corn bread batter.
6. Pour cornbread mixture into hot skillet; bake 20 to 25 minutes.
7. Cornbread is done when bread is golden, top cracks and cornbread pulls away from the sides of the pan.

www.thejoyofsoulfood.com

Buttermilk Cornbread

1 tablespoon vegetable oil
1½ cups white or yellow cornmeal
¼ cup plus 2 tablespoons all-purpose flour
2 teaspoons sugar
1 teaspoon salt
1 teaspoon baking soda
¼ cup vegetable oil
1½ cups buttermilk
2 large eggs

1. Preheat your oven to 400°F
2. Add oil to cast iron skillet and heat in oven for 5-10 minutes do not allow oil to smoke
3. Mix together all dry ingredients
4. Add wet ingredients and mix well by hand.
5. Remove the hot skillet from the oven and carefully pour oil into the batter. Mix well.
6. Pour batter into the skillet and return to oven.
7. Bake until cornbread is golden brown, top cracks and bread begins to pull away from sides of pan.
8. Allow to cool for 5 minutes and serve hot.

Spoon Bread (or corn pudding)

2 boxes Jiffy Corn Bread
8 oz of sour cream
2 eggs
½ cup milk
½ cup + 2 T vegetable oil
1 small can cream corn

1. Preheat oven to 350 degrees
2. Add 2 T of oil to rectangular 9" x 12" Pyrex pan and allow to heat in oven for 5 minutes
3. Combine remaining ingredients in a mixing bowl.
4. Batter will be lumpy
5. Pour batter into heated pan
6. Bake for 40 minutes.
7. Bread is done when top cracks and bread pulls from the sides of the pan.

www.thejoyofsoulfood.com

Joyful Biscuits

5 cups sifted self rising flour
1/3 cup sugar
1 teaspoon baking soda
1 cup shortening
2 cups buttermilk (room temperature only)
2 pkgs dry yeast dissolved in ¼ cup lukewarm water

1. In large bowl, sift together flour sugar and soda
2. Chop in shortening to dry mixture
3. Add buttermilk and dissolved yeast and stir well
4. Keep covered with plastic wrap over bowl in refrigerator 2 hours to overnight(*best)
5. Flour hands, pinch off enough to form a biscuit, place on greased cookie sheet
6. Let rise at room temperature (1 1/2 to 2 hours) *in a warm oven, biscuits will rise in about 30 minutes
7. Bake in preheated oven at 425° for 10-15 minutes until golden brown

www.thejoyofsoulfood.com

Potato Rolls

1 medium potato, peeled and diced
2 cups water
1 (.25 ounce) package active dry yeast
1/4 cup honey
1 tablespoon vegetable oil
1 1/2 teaspoons salt
1 egg, lightly beaten
6 cups all-purpose flour

1. Place potatoes in a small saucepan and cover with water. Bring to a boil. Reduce heat; cover and cook for 10-15 minutes or until tender. Drain, reserving cooking liquid. Set cooking liquid aside to cool to 110 degrees F-115 degrees F. Mash potato (don't add milk or butter); set aside.

2. In a large mixing bowl, dissolve yeast in warm cooking liquid. Add the honey, oil, salt, egg, 4 cups flour and mashed potato. Beat until smooth. Stir in enough remaining flour to form a soft dough.

3. Turn onto a floured surface; knead until smooth and elastic, about 7-8 minutes. Place in a greased bowl, turning once to grease top. Cover and let rise in a warm place until doubled, about 1 hour.

4. Punch dough down. Turn onto a lightly floured surface; divide into 36 pieces. Shape each into a ball. Place in a greased 15-in. x 10-in. x 1-in. baking pan. Cover and let rise until doubled, about 30 minutes.

5. Bake at 375 degrees F for 20-25 minutes or until golden brown. Serve warm.

www.thejoyofsoulfood.com

Cinnamon Rolls

1 package yeast
1 1/8 cups water warm
1 eggs
3/8 cup sugar
3/8 cup butter melted
3/4 teaspoon salt
4 cups flour
FILLING:
1 tablespoon butter
1/2 cup brown sugar
1/4 cup sugar
2 teaspoons cinnamon
1/8 teaspoon salt

1. Dissolve yeast in warm water.
2. Combine beaten eggs, sugar, melted butter, salt and flour.
3. Knead for 5 minutes.
4. Let rise in covered bowl until double (about 90 minutes).
5. While dough is rising, cut 2 tablespoons of butter into 1 cup brown sugar, 1/2 cup white sugar, cinnamon and salt.
6. Roll out dough into 12 x 24 rectangle. Sprinkle evenly with filling mixture, roll dough and cut into 24 even pieces.
7. Place in two 9 x 13 pans and let rise again for another 90 minutes
8. Bake at 375° F for 20 minutes.

www.thejoyofsoulfood.com

Yeast Dinner Rolls

1 cup whole milk
2 pkg. dry yeast
1/2 cup butter + 3 T melted
1/4 to 1 tsp. salt
1/4 cup sugar
2 eggs
4-1/2 to 5 cups all-purpose flour

1. Warm milk in a small saucepan over low heat. 2. Mix 1/3 of the milk with the dry yeast in a small bowl and let sit until bubbly, about 15 minutes.
3. In a large bowl, combine remaining milk, melted butter, salt and sugar and beat until the sugar is dissolved.
4. Add the beaten eggs and bubbly yeast.
5. Add flour, 1/4 cup at a time, beating on high speed mixer. This step should take at least 5 minutes. When the dough gets too stiff to beat, stir in rest of flour by hand, if necessary, to make a soft dough.
6. Turn out onto floured surface and knead for 5 minutes, until smooth and satiny.
7. Place dough in greased bowl, turning in bowl to oil all sides.
8. Cover and let rise in warm place until light and doubled in size, about 1 hour.
9. Punch down the dough and roll out on floured surface to 1/2" thickness.
10. Cut with 3" round cookie cutter. Brush each roll with melted butter and fold in half to make half circles.
11. Pinch edge lightly to hold, so the rolls don't unfold as they rise.
12. Place in 2 greased 13x9" pans, cover, and let rise again until double, about 45 minutes.
13. Bake rolls at 350 degrees F for 20-25 minutes or until golden brown. Remove from pan immediately and brush with 3T freshly melted butter.

www.thejoyofsoulfood.com

Banana Nut Bread

2 cups all-purpose flour
1 teaspoon salt
2 teaspoons baking soda
1 cup (2 sticks) butter or margarine
2 cups granulated sugar
2 cups mashed overripe bananas
4 eggs
11/4 cup chopped walnuts

1. Preheat the oven to 350 degrees F
2. Spray two 9x5 inch loaf pans very liberally.
3. Sift the flour, salt and baking soda into one large bowl.
4. In a separate bowl, blend butter or margarine and sugar until smooth.
5. Stir in the bananas, eggs, and walnuts until well mixed.
6. Combine the wet ingredients into the dry mixture, and stir just until blended. Divide the batter evenly between the two loaf pans.
7. Bake for 60 to 70 minutes until it tests done,
8. Allow loaves to cool in the pans for at least 5 minutes, then turn out onto a cooling rack or plate , and cool completely.

www.thejoyofsoulfood.com

Pancakes

1 1/2 cups all-purpose flour
3 1/2 teaspoons baking powder
1 teaspoon salt
1 tablespoon white sugar
1 1/4 cups milk
1 egg
3 tablespoons butter, melted
1 tsp vanilla
1 tsp cinnamon

1. In a large bowl, sift together the flour, baking powder, salt and sugar. Make a well in the center and pour in the remaining ingredients; mix until smooth.

2. Heat a lightly oiled griddle or frying pan over medium high heat. Pour or scoop the batter onto the griddle, using approximately 1/4 cup for each pancake. Flip when bubbles cover the pancake and the edges are crisp. Serve hot.

Buttermilk Biscuits

2 cups sifted flour
1 tsp salt
2 tsp baking powder
1 Tsp vegetable oil
1/2 tsp baking soda
1/2 cup shortening
3/4 cup buttermilk

1. Sift flour, salt, baking powder, and soda together into mixing bowl.

2. Cut in shortening until mixture resembles coarse crumbs.

3. Add buttermilk all at once, and stir just until dough ball forms.

4. Pat out 1/2 or 1/2-inch thick on lightly floured board, and cut with biscuit cutter.

5. Place on greased baking sheet; brush lightly with melted fat, and bake in a very hot oven (450 degrees F.) about 15 minutes.

www.thejoyofsoulfood.com

Waffles

2 eggs
2 cups all-purpose flour
1 3/4 cups milk
1/2 cup vegetable oil
2 tablespoon white sugar
4 teaspoons baking powder
1/4 teaspoon salt
1 teaspoon vanilla extract
Pecans (optional)
Blueberries (optional)

1. Preheat waffle iron. Beat eggs in large bowl with hand beater until fluffy. Beat in flour, milk, vegetable oil, sugar, baking powder, salt and vanilla, just until smooth.
2. Spray preheated waffle iron with non-stick cooking spray. Pour mix onto hot waffle iron.
3. You may add blueberries OR pecans at this time if desired before closing the waffle iron lid.
4. Cook until golden brown. Serve hot.

www.thejoyofsoulfood.com

Rice Dishes
One dish and easy

Jambalaya

3 cups diced, cooked chicken, turkey, Smoked Sausage
and/or shrimp
2 cups cooked rice
2 cups (No.1 can) tomatoes
1 medium onion, chopped
1/2 green pepper, chopped
2 stalks of celery
3 Tsp butter or olive oil
1/2 tsp salt
Dash of pepper

Season desired meat with Salt and pepper
Sautee meat with onion, green pepper and celery in
butter or oil for 5 minutes. (Note: If using leftovers or just
sausage, seasoning meat may not be required. These
are usually already well seasoned.)
Combine meat and vegetables with rice and
tomatoes, and simmer for 10 minutes.

Add salt and pepper; cover, and simmer for 20 minutes,
adding hot water as needed to keep mixture moist.
Stir occasionally, to prevent mixture from sticking and rice
from overcooking.
Serve hot with corn bread.

Chicken and Rice Casserole

4 chicken breasts
1 can cream of celery soup
1 can cream of chicken soup
1 can cream of mushroom soup
2 stalks celery, diced
1 bay leaf
1 large onion, chopped
1/2 teaspoon Bell's Poultry seasoning
3 cloves garlic, minced
1 cup Minute Rice

1. Mix the cans of soup with the rice at the bottom of the Crockpot. You may substitute the type of soup you use in any combination (for example: 2 cans cream of chicken soup and one can celery soup).
2. Add the diced celery, onion, and garlic and stir. Submerge the chicken in the soup.
3. Turn heat to high for 10 minutes, then reduce to medium and cook for 4-5 hours. Or cook on high for 3-4 hours.

www.thejoyofsoulfood.com

Rice and Black Beans

1 lb dry black beans
1/4 cup olive oil
2 onions, chopped
1 shallot, minced (optional)
2 bell peppers (red or green), chopped
4-5 cloves garlic, minced
1 1/2 teaspoon oregano
1/2 teaspoon paprika
1 packet Goya Sazon (seasoning)
1/4 cup white wine (or wine vinegar)
2 teaspoons salt
1/2 teaspoon black pepper
1/4 teaspoon cayenne pepper (or to taste)
1 teaspoon Frank's Hot Sauce

1. Pick over beans to remove imperfect beans and any foreign matter. Rinse well in cold running water.
2. In a pan, bring beans to a boil in 6-8 cups water. Boil over high heat for 3-4 minutes, then cover and set aside for an hour. Alternatively, boiling can be omitted if beans are soaked overnight.
3. Drain and rinse beans. In a large saucepan, soak beans in 8 cups fresh water. (This time, do not drain.)
4. In a skillet, sauté onion and pepper over medium heat until onions are tender and translucent. Add garlic and oregano when onions begin to color (about 5 minutes). Do not allow garlic to brown. Add remaining ingredients; mix well.
5. Stir mixture into beans in saucepan. Bring to a boil, reduce heat to low. Simmer until beans are tender. Serve over steamed white rice while still hot.
6. Can be prepared in a Crock-Pot. Just soak beans overnight and put everything into the Crock-Pot in the morning. Set on low and cook for 8 hours, or until beans are tender.

www.thejoyofsoulfood.com

Herb Rice

2 cups rice (dry measure)
1/4 cup butter
1/2 onion, diced
4 cups chicken broth
2 tsp parsley
1 tsp minced garlic
½ tsp oregano
1 teaspoon soy sauce

1. In large saucepan, mix butter, onion and rice together;
2. Heat until rice is lightly browned.
3. Add broth, seasoning and soy sauce; bring to boil.
4. Reduce heat to low, cover pan and allow rice to cook/steam for 20 minutes.
5. Remove from heat. Lightly stir to fluff and serve hot.

Red Beans and Rice

1 tbsp. butter
1/2 medium green pepper, chopped (about 1/2 cup)
1/2 medium onion, chopped (about 1/2 cup)
1 can (14 1/2 oz.) beef broth
1 can (15 1/2 oz.) red kidney beans, drained, rinsed
2 cups diced ham or cooked sausage at the same time as
the broth
1 tbsp. Cajun seasoning
2 cups cooked rice, uncooked
Traditional red pepper sauce (optional)

1. Melt butter in large skillet over medium heat. Add bell peppers and onions; cook and stir until crisp-tender.
2. Add broth, beans and hot pepper sauce; stir. Bring to boil.
3. Stir in rice; cover. Remove from heat. Let stand 5 min. Fluff with fork. Serve with pepper sauce, if desired.

www.thejoyofsoulfood.com

Tomatoes and Rice
(Spanish Rice)

2 cups rice (rinsed in 3 waters) see
www.thejoyofsoulfood.com
¼ cup olive oil
1 medium onion
4 cloves garlic
¼ tsp red pepper flakes
¼ cup green, yellow or red pepper finely chopped
4 cups chicken broth
1 can diced tomatoes

1. In large saucepan sauté onions, garlic, peppers and rice in olive oil until onions are translucent.
2. Add remaining ingredients, cover and simmer on low for 20 minutes.
3. Do not lift lid until 20 minutes has passed.
4. Fluff rice and serve hot

Broccoli Cheese Soufflé

2 Tbsp. grated Parmesan cheese
5 Tbsp. butter
5 Tbsp. flour
1 cup evaporated milk
1 cup milk
1/2 tsp. kosher salt
1 tsp. dry mustard
1/2 cup shredded low-fat cheddar cheese
16 oz. frozen broccoli
4 egg yolks, lightly beaten
6 egg whites
1/2 tsp. cream of tartar

1. Preheat oven to 350 degrees F. Spray a 2-quart soufflé dish with nonstick cooking spray. Set aside.
2. Heat the butter in a medium saucepan over medium heat. When the butter is melted, add the flour and stir with a wire whisk. Cook 2-3 minutes, whisking constantly.
3. Pour in the evaporated milk and milk and continue whisking constantly to prevent lumps from forming. Add the kosher salt and dry mustard. Continue whisking until the mixture boils and thickens, about 2 to 4 minutes more
4. Stir in the cheddar cheese and the broccoli. When the cheese has melted, remove from heat.
5. Stir in the eggs, one at a time, until well incorporated.
6. Gently pour the batter into the prepared pan. Bake for a minimum of 30 to 40 minutes or until the soufflé is puffed and golden.

www.thejoyofsoulfood.com

Pasta

Yes, love it too! We just don't use as much oregano.

Chicken Pasta with Sun Dried Tomatoes and Spinach

Ingredients
Chopped chicken 4 chicken breasts cubed
I medium onion finely chopped
3 cloves fresh garlic minced
1 lb fresh raw Baby Spinach leaves
¼ cup Half and half (or regular milk)
1 tsp Garlic powder
1 tsp Seasoned salt
½ tsp Black pepper
Italian Seasonings
Sun dried tomatoes
Flour

1. Prepare pasta according to package instructions add 1 T olive oil to avoid sticking. Do not overcook.
Season the chicken with seasoned salt, garlic, and black pepper and set aside.
2. Add onions to the olive oil in a large frying pan and cook until translucent.
3. Add the chicken and garlic to the onions and allow to cook on medium heat.
7. After 10 minutes, add spinach, broth and sundried tomatoes to the chicken mixture and allow to cook on low.
8. Mix half and half and flour before adding to the other in a small bowl and stir well.
9. Pour flower mixture into chicken and stir to fully combined. Cook for about 3 minutes until you reach your desired consistency.
12. Drain pasta and carefully add to chicken and vegetables Allow flavors to combine stirring carefully. Cook for 3 minutes. If more sauce is desired, add chicken stock.
13. Garnish with fresh parsley and parmesan cheese Optional)

www.thejoyofsoulfood.com

Muscocholli

1 16 oz box muscocholli noodles
1T olive oil
1 lb Lean ground beef
1 medium onion diced
1 tsp garlic
1 tsp seasoned salt
1/2 tsp black pepper
1 28 oz can tomato sauce
1 tsp sugar
½ cup parmesan cheese
1 tsp oregano
½ tsp red pepper flakes (optional)
1 cup Shredded mozzarella cheese

1. Cook pasta according to package instructions.
2. Heat olive oil over medium heat in large skillet. Add ground beef, onion, garlic, salt, and pepper.
3. Brown ground beef and pour off excess oil.
4. Add cooked pasta to beef mixture.
5. Add tomato sauce, sugar, oregano and cheese. Stir thoroughly and allow to cook over low heat for 10 minutes. Add salt and pepper to taste
6. Add pepper flakes if desired and stir thoroughly
7. Garnish with mozzarella cheese and serve.

www.thejoyofsoulfood.com

Macaroni and Cheese

16 oz elbow macaroni
1 small can carnation evaporated milk
1 egg
1t Salt
1t Black Pepper
1t Garlic powder
½ t paprika
2 T Flour
2T butter
1 ½ cup Shredded sharp Cheddar cheese
6 slices American cheese
Cooking spray

Garnish: ½ cup shredded mild cheddar cheese and black pepper

1. Prepare macaroni according to package instructions
2. In sauce pan over medium heat stir together milk, egg, salt, pepper, garlic, paprika, and cheeses.
3. Stir until cheeses melt completely and add flour.
4. Add cooked macaroni to cheese mixture. Mix completely.
5. Spray 9x12 baking pan evenly with non stick cooking spray
6. Pour macaroni mixture into prepared pan.
7. Bake for 20 minutes until bubbly
8. Sprinkle with remaining cheddar cheese, sprinkle lightly with black pepper and bake for 5 additional minutes.
9. Let stand 5-10 minutes before serving.

Pasta Salad

1 box tri-color Rotini pasta
1 sm. red onion
1 sm. yellow pepper
1 sm. red pepper
1 lg. carrot-shredded
1 head of broccoli - finely chopped
1 bottle Wishbone Italian dressing

1. Cook noodles according to box directions and rinse in cold water. Do not overcook.
2. Dice onion, peppers, and carrot into small pieces.
3. Add all veggies to the cooked pasta noodles.
4. Pour dressing over top, using as much or little as you like, to taste.
5. Best if left refrigerated overnight before serving.

Macaroni Salad

2 cups dry elbow macaroni, cooked, rinsed, and drained
1/3 cup diced celery
1/4 cup minced red onion, soaked in cold water for 5
minutes, drained
1 tablespoon minced flat-leaf parsley
1/2 cup diced vine-ripened tomato (optional)
1/2 cup prepared mayonnaise
3/4 teaspoon dry mustard
1 1/2 teaspoons sugar
1 1/2 tablespoons cider vinegar
3 tablespoons sour cream
1/2 teaspoon kosher salt, plus more to taste
Freshly ground black pepper

1. In a large bowl combine the macaroni, celery, onion, parsley and tomato, if using.
2. In a small bowl, whisk together the mayonnaise, mustard, sugar, vinegar, sour cream and salt.
3. Pour the dressing over the salad and stir to combine. Season with salt and pepper to taste.
4. Serve cold.
5. Store covered in the refrigerator, for up to 3 days.

Lasagna

1 16 oz box lasagna noodles
2 T olive oil
1 lb Lean ground beef or ground turkey
1 medium onion diced
½ bell pepper finely chopped
4 cloves garlic
1 tsp seasoned salt
1/2 tsp black pepper
1 28 oz can tomato sauce
1 tsp sugar
1 tsp Italian seasonings
½ tsp red pepper flakes (optional)
2 bay leaves
1 cup Shredded mozzarella cheese
1 cup parmesan cheese
1 cup shredded cheddar cheese

1. Cook pasta according to package instructions.
2. Heat olive oil over medium heat in large skillet. Add meat, onion, and bell pepper,
3. Brown meat and season with garlic, salt, and pepper.
4. Pour off excess oil.
5. Add tomato sauce, sugar, oregano, seasonings, and to meat. Stir thoroughly and allow to cook over low heat for 10 minutes. Add salt and pepper to taste
6. Pour light layer of sauce to bottom of 9x12 baking pan.
7. Layer lasagna noodle, meat sauce shredded cheese, then parmesan cheese.
8. Repeat layers 2 more times.
9. Bake for 30 minutes at 350°
10. Allow to cool for 5-10 minutes
11. Garnish with mozzarella cheese and serve hot.

www.thejoyofsoulfood.com

Spaghetti with Meat Sauce

1 16 oz box spaghetti noodles
2 T olive oil
1 lb Lean ground beef or ground turkey
1 medium onion diced
½ bell pepper finely chopped
4 cloves garlic
1 tsp seasoned salt
1/2 tsp black pepper
1 28 oz can tomato sauce
1 tsp sugar
1 tsp Italian seasonings
½ tsp red pepper flakes (optional)
2 bay leaves
1 cup parmesan cheese

1. Cook pasta according to package instructions. Do not overcook.
2. Heat olive oil over medium heat in large skillet. Add meat, onion, and bell pepper,
3. Brown meat and season with garlic, salt, and pepper.
4. Pour off excess oil.
5. Add tomato sauce, sugar, oregano, and seasonings to meat. Stir thoroughly and allow to cook over low heat for 10 minutes. Add salt and pepper to taste
6. Drain and rinse noodles return to pot, stir in one tablespoon of olive oil to avoid sticking and cover.
7. To serve, add desired amount of pasta to plate, top with desired amount of meat sauce and garnish with parmesan cheese.

Shrimp Alfredo

1 16 oz box of linguini
2 T Olive Oil
1 stick butter
1 lb shrimp
4 cloves of garlic
1 medium onion finely chopped
2 cans of chopped clams with sauce
1 bunch of fresh parsley finely chopped
1 tsp oregano
2 T sour cream

1. Cook pasta according to package instructions. Do not overcook.
2. Heat olive oil and butter over medium heat in large skillet. Add shrimp, onion, and garlic. Cook for 5 minutes.
3. Add remaining ingredients and simmer together for 10 minutes.
4. Stir linguini into shrimp sauce and allow flavors to combine for 5 minutes.
5. Serve hot and garnish with parmesan cheese and parsley.

Soups
To warm the heart and the body

Roasted Butternut Squash Soup

1 large butternut squash
1 stick (1/2 cup) salted sweet butter
2 T extra-virgin olive oil
½ cup diced onion
¼ cup diced celery
½ t garlic powder
¼ cinnamon stick
Sea Salt and Freshly ground pepper
4 cups chicken stock or broth
¼ cup molasses (or granulated sugar)
½ cup half and half

1. Cut the squash in half lengthwise and scoop out seeds
2. Brush cut side with olive oil and sprinkle generously with salt and pepper
3. Place face down on baking dish and bake for 1 hour or until squash is soft
4. In large saucepan, sauté onion celery , garlic powder and cinnamon stick in butter until onion becomes translucent.
5. Add chicken stock, molasses (or sugar) , to broth
6. Once cool enough to handle, easily peel the skin off the squash and in batches place in food processor or blender until smooth.
7. Pour blended squash into sauce pot, add half and half stir and simmer
8. Serve immediately. Refrigerate up to 5 days freeze for up to 2 months.

www.thejoyofsoulfood.com

Louisiana Chicken Gumbo

6 large boneless skinless chicken breast
4 T butter
1 lb smoked sausage
1 medium onion, sliced
3 stalks celery sliced
1 1/2 tsp salt
1 quart hot water
2 cups sliced okra
1 sprig fresh or 1 tsp dry thyme
1 can of oysters (optional)
1/16 tsp cayenne pepper
Old Bay Seasoning (to taste)
1 Tsp file' or 3 Tsp sassafras leaves
Cooked rice (according to package instructions)

1. Cube chicken breasts
2. Sauté chicken in butter in heavy frying pan until browned, turning frequently.
3. Add sausage onion and celery, and sauté about 10 minutes.
4. Add salt and water; bring to a boil, and simmer about 1 1/2 hours, or until chicken is tender.
5. Add okra and thyme, and simmer 1/2 hour longer, or until okra is tender.
7. Add oysters and additional seasoning if needed.
9. Just before serving stir in file'
10. Serve at once with pre cooked steamed rice

For seafood gumbo:
add 1 lb small shrimp with tails removed when you add the oysters.

www.thejoyofsoulfood.com

Vegetable Soup*

4 cups chicken broth/stock **or**
4 cups of water +4 chicken bouillon cubes
2 Medium Carrots sliced
2 stalks of Celery sliced
1 medium Onion finely chopped
2 cloves garlic minced or 1 tsp dry minced garlic
½ cup fresh or frozen Corn
½ cup fresh or frozen string beans
Can Diced Tomatoes
½ tsp Garlic powder
½ tsp Onion powder
½ tsp Seasoned Salt
¼ tsp Pepper
2 Green Onions-thinly sliced
2 bay leaves

1. Add all ingredients to a large stock pot,

2. Cover with tight fitting lid and cook on medium until carrots are done, about 20 minutes

3. Remove bay leaves and serve hot.

4. Salt and Pepper to taste

*Carrots, Onions and Celery are required. Any other vegetable-- fresh or frozen, in any combination may be used in this soup. There really are no rules
www.thejoyofsoulfood.com

Potato Soup

4 medium potatoes peeled and diced
4 cups chicken broth/stock **or**
4 cups of water +4 chicken bouillon cubes
½ tsp Garlic powder
½ tsp Onion powder
½ tsp Seasoned Salt
¼ tsp Pepper
2 Green Onions-thinly sliced
1 bay leaf
1 cup heavy cream

1. Add all ingredients except cream to a large stock pot,

2. cover with tight fitting lid and cook on medium until potatoes begin to fall apart, about 20 minutes

3. Add cream, stir and cook for 10 minutes

4. Remove bay leaf and serve hot.

5. Salt and Pepper to taste

www.thejoyofsoulfood.com

Black Bean Soup

1 lb dried black beans or 2 16-oz cans black beans, rinsed
and drained
1 Tbsp canola oil
1 medium onion, chopped
4 cloves garlic, minced
1 carrot, shredded
1 green bell pepper, seeded and chopped
8 cups water
4 oz smoked turkey breast, diced
2 tsp oregano
1/2 tsp cumin
1/2 tsp pepper
1 tsp salt

1. If using dried beans, soak them in water overnight. The next day, drain the beans.

2. In a large soup pot, heat the oil over medium heat. Add half the onion and all the garlic, carrot, and green pepper. Sauté' until vegetable are soft. Stir in the beans and water. Add the turkey, oregano, cumin, and pepper.

3. Cover and simmer for 30 minutes or until the beans are tender, stirring occasionally. Add the salt and lemon juice. Top with chopped onion to serve.

Tomato Soup with Basil

2 (28 ounce) cans crushed tomatoes
1 (14.5 ounce) can chicken broth
1 tsp garlic powder
1 onion powder
¼ tsp salt
¼ tsp white pepper
18 fresh basil leaves, minced
1 teaspoon sugar
1 cup half and half or whipping cream
1/2 cup butter or margarine

1. In a large saucepan, add tomatoes, broth garlic and onion powder, salt and pepper. Bring to a boil.
2. Reduce heat; cover and simmer for 10 minutes.
3. Add basil and sugar. Reduce heat to low;
4. Stir in cream and butter. Cook until butter is melted.

Homemade Chicken Soup

4 large chicken breasts cubed
4 cups chicken broth/stock **or**
4 cups of water +4 chicken bouillon cubes
2 Medium Carrots sliced
2 stalks of Celery sliced
1 medium Onion finely chopped
2 cloves garlic minced or 1 tsp dry minced garlic
½ tsp Garlic powder
½ tsp Onion powder
½ tsp Seasoned Salt
¼ tsp Pepper
2 Green Onions-thinly sliced
2 bay leaves
Noodles (Optional)*

1. Add all ingredients to a large stock pot,
2. Cover with tight fitting lid and cook on medium until chicken is fully cooked, about 30 minutes
3. Remove bay leaves and serve hot.
4. Salt and Pepper to taste

*If you want noodles or rice in your soup, cook them according to package directions in a separate pot and add a small amount to the chicken soup just before serving.

www.thejoyofsoulfood.com

Corn Chowder

1/2 cup diced bacon
4 medium potatoes, peeled and chopped
1 medium onion, chopped
2 cups water
3 cups frozen corn
½ tsp onion powder
½ tsp garlic powder
1½ tsp seasoned salt
¼ tsp black pepper
2 cups half-and-half or whipping cream
1 bay leaf

1. Fry bacon in a large pot over medium-high heat until crisp.
2. Remove fried bacon and crumble into separate bowl, Reserve about 2 tablespoons bacon drippings in the pot.
3. Add potatoes and onion into the pot, return the crumbled bacon and cook in the reserved drippings. For 5 minutes.
4. Pour in the water, and stir in corn. Add all seasonings and bay leaf and bring to a boil; reduce heat to low, and cover pot. Simmer 20 minutes, stirring frequently, until potatoes are tender.
5. Warm the half-and-half in a small saucepan until it bubbles. Remove from heat before it boils, and mix into the chowder just before serving.

www.thejoyofsoulfood.com

Clam Chowder

1/2 cup diced ham
4 medium potatoes, peeled and chopped
1 medium onion, chopped
1 cup water
3 -10 oz cans minced clams with juice
½ tsp onion powder
½ tsp garlic powder
1½ tsp seasoned salt
¼ tsp black pepper
1 bay leaf
2 cups half-and-half or whipping cream
1-2 T flour

1. Fry ham in a large pot over medium-high heat until browned.
2. Add potatoes and onion into the pot, Cook for 5 minutes. Stirring to avoid sticking
3. Pour in the water, and clams with juice. Add all seasonings and bay leaf and bring to a boil; reduce heat to low, and cover pot. Simmer 20 minutes, stirring frequently, until potatoes are tender.
4. Warm the half-and-half in a small saucepan until it bubbles add flour and stir to combine. Remove from heat before it boils, and mix into the chowder . Once fully mixed, Serve hot.

www.thejoyofsoulfood.com

Beef and Vegetable Soup*

1 cup thinly sliced beef roast-any cut
4 cups beef broth/stock **or**
4 cups of water +4 beef bouillon cubes
2 Medium Carrots sliced
2 stalks of Celery sliced
1 medium Onion finely chopped
2 cloves garlic minced or 1 tsp dry minced garlic
½ cup fresh or frozen Corn
½ cup fresh or frozen string beans
Can Diced Tomatoes
½ tsp Garlic powder
½ tsp Onion powder
½ tsp Seasoned Salt
¼ tsp Pepper
2 Green Onions-thinly sliced
2 bay leaves

1. Add all ingredients to a large stock pot,
2. Cover with tight fitting lid and cook on medium until carrots are done, about 20 minutes
3. Remove bay leaves and serve hot.
4. Salt and Pepper to taste.

www.thejoyofsoulfood.com

Chili

1 pound lean ground beef
2 16 oz cans diced tomatoes
1 medium onion chopped
1 bell pepper chopped
Chili powder
Seasoned salt
Red pepper flakes
Red beans
Garlic powder
Onion powder
Bay leaf
Cumin
Oregano
Hot sauce (optional)

1. Brown ground beef in a large pot. Add onions and cook until translucent.
2. Pour in tomatoes water and seasonings.
3. Stir and allow to cook for 30 minutes.
4. Pour liquid off canned beans and add to chili
5. Serve hot, garnished with shredded cheddar cheese.

Vegetables

Where collard greens are king and pot liquor is the prince

Traditional Collard Greens

2 lb collard greens
4 cups water
4 chicken bouillon cubes
1 medium onions, chopped
3 whole garlic cloves, crushed
1 tsp red pepper flakes (optional)
1 tsp black pepper
1 whole bell pepper-diced
1/4 cup olive oil.

1. Place washed and cut collard greens in a large stockpot (for video instruction, visit www.thejoyofsoulfood.com).
2. Add all remaining ingredients and just cover with water (do not add too much water).
3. Cook over medium heat until tender.
4. Stir occasionally. For tender greens, expect to cook for about 3 hours.
5. Serve with sliced tomatoes, sliced onions, yellow pepper rings and cornbread.

www.thejoyofsoulfood.com

Fried Corn

8 ears of sweet corn , shucked and silked
1medium green bell pepper, finely chopped
1 medium onion finely chopped
1/2 cup all-purpose flour
1 tablespoon sugar
1 stick butter
seasoned salt and pepper to taste

1. Slice corn off the cob into a large bowl.
2. Sauté onion, pepper in butter in large skillet over medium heat.
3. Add Corn to skillet with all juices
4. Add flour seasoned salt and pepper
5. Cover tightly with lid and continue cooking over medium heat for 5 minutes. Corn will become tender and flour will begin to brown.

Dried Beans/Peas with Turkey

1 lb dried beans or peas
2 qt water
1 medium onion, chopped
1 lb smoked turkey breast, chopped
1/2 t Seasoned Salt
1/2 t Black Pepper
1/2 t Granulated Garlic
1/2 t Dried Onion Flakes
Red Pepper Flakes to taste (optional)

1. Soak the beans or peas overnight in cold water in large bowl, covering the top with 1/2 inch of water or boil for 2 minutes and then soak for 1 hour. Drain.

2. Place the soaked and drained peas in a large stockpot and add the water, onion, smoked turkey, and red pepper flakes. Simmer for 2 hours or until the peas are soft.

3. Add all seasonings and simmer for 20 minutes.

Serve with steamed rice

www.thejoyofsoulfood.com

Stir Fried Greens

(May substitute Collards, Spinach, Mustard, Kale, Callaloo, Cabbage or any greens combination)

3T Olive Oil
1 medium Onion dices
½ large bell pepper (green, yellow, red or orange)diced
4 Garlic Cloves minced
2T Soy Sauce
1t Seasoned Salt
1t Garlic
½ t Black Pepper
½ t Onion Powder
¼ t Red pepper flakes (optional)
½ t oregano (optional)

1. Wash greens thoroughly, remove all stems and drain completely.
2. Heat oil in heavy skillet with tight fitting lid over medium heat.
3. Add onions, garlic and peppers and cook until onions and peppers begin to wilt
4. Add prepared greens to skillet.
5. Season evenly with soy sauce and spices.
6. Toss gently and cover with lid. Cook for about 3 minutes over medium heat.
7. Stir greens to combine ingredients evenly and cook until desired tenderness (about an additional 3-4 minutes).
8. Serve while hot.

www.thejoyofsoulfood.com

Black Eyes Peas

1 lb dried black-eyed peas
6 cups water
1 medium onion, chopped
1 lb smoked turkey breast, chopped
1/2 t Seasoned Salt
1/2 t Black Pepper
1/2 t Granulated Garlic
1/2 t Dried Onion Flakes
Red Pepper Flakes to taste (optional)

1. Soak the black-eyed peas overnight in cold water in large bowl, covering the top with 1/2 inch of water or boil for 2 minutes and then soak for 1 hour. Drain.

2. Place the soaked and drained peas in a large stockpot and add the 6 cups of water, onion, smoked turkey, and red pepper flakes. Simmer for 2 hours or until the peas are soft.

3. Add all seasonings and simmer for 20 minutes.

Serve with corn bread

Candied Yams

4-6 medium sweet potatoes peeled and sliced in 1/2 inch segments
1 stick of sweetened salted butter
1/4 tsp nutmeg
1/4 tsp ginger
1/2 tsp cinnamon
1/2 tsp real vanilla extract
1/2 cup brown sugar

1. Boil whole potatoes with skin on until they pierce easily with a fork.

2. Allow potatoes to cool. Then peel easily with your hands and cut into 1/2 inch medallions

3. In separate pot melt butter and brown sugar together add all seasonings

4. Add Sweet Potato medallions and cover with brown sugar cinnamon mixture

5. Serve Hot

Baked French Fries

4 large potatoes Cut into fries
Season Salt
Black Pepper
Granulated Garlic
Onion Powder
Cooking Spray

1. Peel potatoes and cut into fries.

2. Spray baking pan with non stick cooking spray

3. Spread potatoes evenly on cooking sheet.

4. Sprinkle seasoning evenly over potatoes.

5. Turn potatoes and spray potatoes lightly with cooking spray

6. Season opposite side of potatoes with seasonings

7. Bake at 450° for 15-20 minutes

8. Turn fries over and continue to cut until brown on all sides.

Baked Sweet Potato Medallions

4 large sweet potatoes
Ground Cinnamon
4T Butter
½ cup packed brown sugar
½ cup chopped pecans

1. Boil whole potatoes in large sauce pan until completely done (pierces easily with fork).

2. Preheat oven to 350°

3. Drain hot water from potatoes and cover with cold water.

4. Allow to cool until potatoes handle comfortably with hands.

5. Peel boiled potatoes and slice into ½ inch thick slices.

6. Spray baking pan evenly with cooking spray

7. Arrange medallions on baking sheet and pray potatoes lightly with cooking spray.

8. Sprinkle cinnamon evenly over sweet potatoes

9. Crumble brown sugar evenly over potatoes

10. Sprinkle pecans evenly over potatoes

11. Drizzle butter evenly over potato slices

12. Bake on medium rack until sugar becomes bubbly.

13. Remove from oven and allow to cool slightly.

www.thejoyofsoulfood.com

Fried Green Tomatoes (or Okra)

4 large green tomatoes
2 eggs
1/2 cup milk
1 cup all-purpose flour
1/2 cup cornmeal
1/2 cup panko bread crumbs
1 teaspoon seasoned salt
1/4 teaspoon ground black pepper
1 quart vegetable oil for frying

1. Slice tomatoes 1/2 inch thick. Discard the ends.

2. Whisk eggs and milk together in a medium-size bowl. Scoop flour onto a plate. Mix cornmeal, bread crumbs and salt and pepper on another plate. Dip tomatoes into flour to coat. Then dip the tomatoes into milk and egg mixture. Dredge in breadcrumbs to completely coat.

3. In a large skillet, pour vegetable oil (enough so that there is 1/2 inch of oil in the pan) and heat over a medium heat. Place tomatoes into the frying pan in batches of 4 or 5, depending on the size of your skillet. Do not crowd the tomatoes, they should not touch each other. When the tomatoes are browned, flip and fry them on the other side. Drain them on paper towels.

www.thejoyofsoulfood.com

Fried Eggplant or Summer Squash

1 large eggplant , or 1 pound summer squash or Zucchini
4 T Olive Oil + 1T butter
Seasoned salt
Black Pepper
Garlic Powder
Seasoned flour or Panko bread crumbs

1. Wash squash and cut into 1/2-inch slices.

2. Dip slices in well-seasoned flour or crumbs, and fry in oil at medium heat for about 10 minutes, or until crisp and browned, turning occasionally.

3. Allow to drain on paper towels

4. Serve hot.

Sautéed Eggplant or Summer Squash

1 large eggplant , or 1 pound summer squash or Zucchini
1 small onion
2T Olive Oil + 1T butter
seasoned salt
pepper
garlic powder
1 T flour

1. Heat oil and butter in medium skillet until butter melts.

2. Add all ingredients except for flour and cook until squash is tender and onions are translucent.

3. Sprinkle with flour and fry until flour starts to turn brown, stirring frequently.

4. Serve Hot.

Sweet Potato Soufflé

4 medium sweet potatoes
2 Tbsp sugar
1/2 cup brown sugar
1 tsp nutmeg
½ tsp cinnamon
1/2 cup evaporated milk
1/3 cup butter
1 egg
1/2 cup chopped pecans
1/2 tsp salt

Nonstick cooking spray

1. Peel and boil the sweet potatoes. Heat the oven to 350 F.

2. Drain and mash the sweet potatoes. Place them in a large bowl and add all ingredients. Stir well.

3. Spray a casserole dish with nonstick cooking spray. Place the sweet potatoes in the casserole dish, sprinkle with pecans and bake for 30 minutes.

www.thejoyofsoulfood.com

Candied Yams

4-6 medium sweet potatoes peeled and sliced in 1/2 inch
segments
1 stick of sweetened salted butter
1/4 tsp nutmeg
1/4 tsp ginger
1/2 tsp cinnamon
1/2 tsp real vanilla extract
1/2 cup brown sugar

1. Boil whole potatoes with skin on until they pierce easily with a fork.

2. Allow potatoes to cool. Then peel easily with your hands and cut into 1/2 inch medallions

3. In separate pot melt butter and brown sugar together add all seasonings

4. Add Sweet Potato medallions and cover with brown sugar cinnamon mixture

5. Serve Hot,

www.thejoyofsoulfood.com

Southern Potato Salad

4 large potatoes
½ t Seasoned Salt
½ t Black Pepper
½ t Granulated Garlic
½ Green Bell Pepper finely chopped
½ medium sized onion
2 Boiled Eggs diced
6 Hamburger Dill Pickle slices chopped finely + 2 T pickle juice
1 T Pickled Relish
2T Mustard
3T Light Mayonnaise (May substitute salad dressing)
Garnish: Paprika and one sliced boiled egg

1. Boil whole potatoes in large sauce pan until completely done (pierces easily with fork).
2. Drain hot water from potatoes and cover with cold water.
3. Allow to cool until potatoes handle comfortably with hands.
4. Dice all remaining vegetables
5. Peel boiled potatoes and dice into ½ inch cubes.
6. Combine Potatoes, eggs, and vegetables in medium sized mixing bowl.
7. Sprinkle seasonings (except paprika) evenly over top of potato mixture.
8. Add mustard and mayonnaise and stir well.
9. Taste the potato salad. If you prefer more of any seasoning, add it now. or if you
10. prefer more moisture add more mayo now.
11. Smooth finished salad with back of spoon.
12. Arrange sliced egg over top as desired.
13. Sprinkle top with paprika

www.thejoyofsoulfood.com

Garlic Mashed Potatoes

2-1/2 lb. baking potatoes (about 7), peeled, quartered
4 cloves garlic, minced
1 tub (8 oz.)PHILADELPHIA Cream Cheese Spread
2 Tbsp. butter
1 tsp. salt
½ tsp garlic powder
½ tsp white pepper

1. Cook potatoes and garlic in boiling water in large saucepan 20 min. or until potatoes are tender; drain.

2. Mash potatoes until smooth.

3. Stir in remaining ingredients until well blended.

www.thejoyofsoulfood.com

Meat

Because its meat!

Chicken Pasta with Sun Dried Tomatoes and Spinach

Ingredients

Chopped chicken 4 chicken breasts cubed
I medium onion finely chopped
3 cloves fresh garlic minced
1 lb fresh raw Baby Spinach leaves
¼ cup Half and half (or regular milk)
1 tsp Garlic powder
1 tsp Seasoned salt
½ tsp Black pepper
Italian Seasonings
Sun dried tomatoes
Flour

1. Prepare pasta according to package instructions add 1 T olive oil to avoid sticking. Do not overcook.
Season the chicken with seasoned salt, garlic, and black pepper and set aside.
2. Add onions to the olive oil in a large frying pan and cook until translucent.
3. Add the chicken and garlic to the onions and allow to cook on medium heat.
7. After 10 minutes, add spinach, broth and sundried tomatoes to the chicken mixture and allow to cook on low.
8. Mix half and half and flour before adding to the other in a small bowl and stir well.
9. Pour flower mixture into chicken and stir to fully combined. Cook for about 3 minutes until you reach your desired consistency.
12. Drain pasta and carefully add to chicken and vegetables Allow flavors to combine stirring carefully. Cook for 3 minutes. If more sauce is desired, add chicken stock.
13. Garnish with fresh parsley and parmesan cheese

Chicken Fricassee with Rice

1 stewing chicken, (3 pounds)
1 quart water
1 onion
1/2 bay leaf
1 tsp salt
Seasoned flour
2 slices salt pork, cut fine
3 Tsp butter or margarine
3 Tsp flour
1 1/2 cup stock
1/2 cup cream
3 cups boiled rice

1. Disjoint chicken

2. Cook gently with water, onion, bay leaf, and salt for 1 1/2 to 2 hours or until tender.

3. Remove chicken, roll in seasoned flour, and fry until brown with salt pork and butter.

4. Remove chicken, add flour to pan fat, and stir until smooth; then stir in chicken stock and cream, and simmer until thick and creamy, stirring occasionally.

5. Season to taste.

6. Place chicken on platter and pour gravy over it.

7. Surround with border of boiled rice.

www.thejoyofsoulfood.com

Classic Fried Chicken

1 whole chicken cut into pieces
Seasoned Salt
Black Pepper
Garlic Powder
Onion Powder
1 T vinegar
Oil Mixture: Vegetable or Peanut Oil + ½ stick butter

Flour Mixture: 2 cups of flour + 1t seasoned salt +1 t black pepper + 1t garlic powder

1. Pour oil into large Cast Iron Skillet until one half full. Heat on medium.
2. In a glass or plastic bowl add vinegar, add chicken pieces and sprinkle all sides evenly with seasonings, set aside.
3. Prepare Flour mixture with seasonings in 1 gallon zippered freezer bag. Shake to combine.
4. Add Chicken pieces one at a time to flour mixture, shake to coat.
5. Shake excess flour from chicken and carefully place in hot oil/butter mixture
6. Fry until golden brown. Make sure oil does not begin to smoke. Do not turn up heat.
7. Turn until browned completely on all sides. Thoroughly fried chicken will not appear red anywhere near the bone.

Curried Chicken

4 large Chicken Breasts cubed
4T Olive Oil
1 t Kosher Sea Salt
½ t White Pepper
4 Garlic Cloves- sliced
1 Bell Pepper (yellow or orange)
1 medium Onion
1 bay leaf
2 T Curried Powder
2 medium Potatoes cubed
2 cup water

1. In large skillet over medium heat, heat olive oil.
2. Add onion, garlic, pepper and sauté until onions are translucent
3. Add curry powder to oil mixture and cook until curry is very fragrant about 2-3 minutes.
4. Add chicken, potatoes and water
5. Cover tightly and cook until chicken and potatoes are thoroughly cooked. Potatoes will pierce easily with potatoes and chicken should not be pink.
6. Discard Bay Leaf
7. Taste curry and add more salt if desired
8. Serve over steamed rice.

www.thejoyofsoulfood.com

Paprika Chicken

Salt
Pepper
Granulated Garlic
2 whole chickens
Paprika
Flour
4T Butter

1. Preheat oven to 350°
2. Cut up 1 whole chicken
3. Season the pieces generously by sprinkling paprika, salt, pepper, and garlic to each side of each piece
4. Add just enough water to cover the bottom of the pan. Arrange chicken on baking dish.
5. Sprinkle the chicken with a very light dusting of flour and dot the chicken pieces with small squares of butter.
6. Cover Baking Dish with aluminum foil, crimp foil to seal edges tightly.
7. Bake in oven at 350° for 40 minutes.
8. Remove Aluminum foil and allow chicken to brown (10-15 minutes). Chicken is done when the meat starts to fall away from the bone.

Panko Chicken Tenders

1 lb Chicken Tenders
1 cup Peanut Oil (or vegetable oil)
1 cup Flour
1 14oz bag Panko Bread Crumbs
1 Egg
1 cup Milk
Salt and Pepper to taste
1/3 cup Honey
3 T Soy Sauce
3T water
1 t Garlic Powder
¼ t red pepper flakes (optional) only if you like spicy food

1. Heat oil in large frying pan or deep fryer to 450°. In a separate saucepan, combine honey, garlic, soy sauce and pepper flakes, heat on low.
2. Salt and pepper the chicken tenders in a bowl and set aside.
3. Whisk egg and milk together in a separate bowl.
4. In a gallon size freezer bag, shake chicken tenders in flour. Shake off excess flour.
5. Dip lightly floured tenders into egg/milk mixture.
6. Drop coated tender into I gallon size freezer bag with Panko Bread Crumbs and shake.
7. Fry coated tenders in heated oil until golden brown.
8. Gently shake off excess oil and coat fried tender in honey ginger sauce.

If desired, allow to drain on cooling rack or serve immediately.

www.thejoyofsoulfood.com

Hot Wings

1 tsp seasoned salt
1/2 teaspoon garlic powder
1/2 teaspoon black pepper
20 chicken wings divided
1/2 cup melted butter

1/2 cup hot pepper sauce (such as Frank's RedHot®,
Louisiana Red or Red Devil <u>not</u> Tabasco)

1. Fill a 10" cast iron skillet half full with vegetable oil and allow to heat on medium.
2. Sprinkle wing parts with salt, garlic powder and pepper, covering generously.
3. Fry wings in hot oil until fully cooked and golden brown.
4. Cook wings for 10-12 minutes- wings will not be red on inside
5. In a large mixing bowl, whisk together melted butter and hot sauce.
6. Toss hot fully cooked wings in pepper sauce and serve with ranch dressing, fresh carrots and celery sticks.

Grilled Smoked Wings

3 pounds Chicken wings
3 cloves Garlic
1 tablespoon grated ginger
1 tablespoon honey
3/4 cup soy sauce
1/2 cup water
1 cup brown sugar
2T vinegar
1 T olive oil

1. Light charcoal in grill and allow coals to burn until they turn white.
2. In a food processor, add all ingredients except for chicken. Process for 20 to 30 seconds to blend.
3. Pour the marinade in a 9-by-13-inch baking pan, and add the chicken wings. Drizzle the marinade over all the wings. Cover and refrigerate for at least 2 hours, rotating the chicken wings at least once.
4. Place wings on grill and cook thoroughly turn until completely cooked. Meat will begin to pull away from the bone.

Serve hot

www.thejoyofsoulfood.com

Creole Fish and Okra

1 medium sliced onion
4 cloves garlic
3T Olive oil
1lb sliced Okra
1 T Oregano
Seasoned salt
Black pepper
5 white fish filets (like tilapia or catfish)
1 large can of chopped tomatoes

1. Heat oil in a four qt saucepan
2. Sautee onions and garlic in olive oil
3. Add okra, oregano, salt, pepper and tomatoes.
4. Stir to combine.
5. Add fish to top of vegetables.
6. Cover with top and steam for 10 minutes.
7. Stir all ingredients together cook another 5 minutes
8. Serve over rice.

www.thejoyofsoulfood.com

Pecan Panko Tilapia

1 pound Tilapia filets
Lawry's seasoned Salt to taste
1 14 oz bag Panko Bread Crumbs
½ cup crushed pecans
Pam spray
2 T Parsley
1 t Garlic Powder
3 T Olive Oil

1. In a gallon freezer bag, combine panko bread crumbs crushed pecans, parsley and 1 t of seasoned salt. Shake together and set aside
2. Coat bottom of 9x12 baking dish with olive oil
3. Wash Tilapia filets and season with salt, pepper and garlic powder
4. Spray each filet with cooking spray
5. Coat filets, one at a time, in bread crumb mixture and lay each filet in oiled baking dish
6. Bake filets at 350 ° for 20 minutes or until golden brown.
7. Enjoy immediately.

www.thejoyofsoulfood.com

Cajun Boiled Fish

2 to 3 pounds fish filets- fish filet such as tilapia, redfish, red
snapper, or halibut
1 quart boiling water
1 carrot, sliced
1/4 cup celery leaves
2 Tsp vinegar or lemon juice
1 clove garlic or small onion, sliced
1 sprig thyme
1 bay leaf
4 whole cloves
1 tsp salt

1. Heat water, vegetables, and seasonings to boiling point, and simmer for 10 minutes.

2. Carefully add filets to water and simmer for about 10 minutes, according to thickness of fish.

3. Fish is done when it flakes easily

4. Use large spatula to remove filets whole

5. Place on hot platter; garnish as desired, serve with rice and broth.

www.thejoyofsoulfood.com

Fried Catfish

1 large egg
1/3 cup milk
½ cup cornmeal
½ cup flour
11/2 t seasoned salt
¼ t onion powder
¼ t garlic powder
½ t black pepper
Optional- 1 to 2 T Louisiana Red Hot Sauce
1 cup peanut oil
4-6 Catfish Filets (about 6 oz each)

1. In a shallow bowl whisk egg, milk and if desired, hot sauce.
2. In a 1 gallon freezer bag, combine all dry ingredients and shake to mix.
3. In a large cast iron skillet, heat peanut oil to 350° or until very hot but not smoking.
4. Dip Fish fillets in egg mixture, then shake in the dry mixture 1-2 at a time.
5. Gently transfer fish into hot oil and fry for about 5 minutes each side.
6. Remove fish with slotted spatula and allow to drain on paper towels.
7. Enjoy immediately

www.thejoyofsoulfood.com

Fried Shrimp

1 large egg
1/3 cup milk
½ cup cornmeal
½ cup flour
1 1/2 t seasoned salt
¼ t onion powder
¼ t garlic powder
½ t black pepper
Optional- 1 to 2 T Louisiana Red Hot Sauce
1 cup peanut oil
1 pound of raw, peeled and deveined shrimp with tail

1. In a shallow bowl whisk egg, milk and if desired, hot sauce.

2. In a 1 gallon freezer bag, combine all dry ingredients and shake to mix.

3. In a large cast iron skillet, heat peanut oil to 350° or until very hot but not smoking

4. Dip shrimp in egg mixture, then shake in the dry mixture 6-8 at a time.

5. Gently transfer shrimp into hot oil and fry for about 3 minutes each side.

6. Remove shrimp with slotted spatula and allow to drain on paper towels.

7. Enjoy immediately

www.thejoyofsoulfood.com

Salmon Croquette

1 15 oz can salmon (or tuna or mackerel), drained
1 medium onion, diced
1/2 medium green bell pepper, diced
1 Tbsp chopped fresh parsley
1 egg
2 T flour
1/2 t seasoned salt
1/4 tsp pepper
Dash of Louisiana Hot Sauce (optional)
2 Tbsp olive oil

1. Discard juice from can of salmon
1. In a medium bowl, break the salmon into small pieces with a fork. Remove the bones and skin.
2. Add the onion, bell pepper, parsley, egg, flour, hot sauce and seasoning.
3. Form the mixture into patties.
4. Heat the oil in a medium skillet and cook the patties over medium heat.
5. Brown for 3 -4 minutes on each side and serve.
6. Serve with rice, biscuits and mango chutney or preserves

Mango Chutney
1 whole ripe mango diced
¼ cup finely diced red onion

Combine and set aside. Serve with biscuits and salmon patties.

www.thejoyofsoulfood.com

Grilled Salmon with Honey Mustard Glaze

1 large Salmon Filet with skin on one side
1t Old Bay Seasoning
1t granulated garlic
Black Pepper to taste
¼ cup mayonnaise (not sandwich spread)
1T Balsamic Vinegar
3T Olive Oil

1. Lay filet, skin side down on heavy aluminum foil.
2. Combine all other above ingredients in small bowl. Mix well.
3. Spread Mayo sauce over flesh side of salmon.
4. Close Aluminum Foil over fish sealing tightly.
5. Cook over medium heat in charcoal grill for 15 minutes.
6. Add honey mustard sauce

Honey Mustard Sauce
3T Honey
1T Dry Mustard
¼ cup packed brown sugar

1. Combine all ingredients in small bowl.
2. After Salmon has cooked for 15 minutes, carefully open aluminum foil with protective gloves and long grill tools.
3. Leave foil open and Spread fish with honey mustard sauce.
4. Cook fish in open foil until bubbly, about 5 minutes.
5. Serve immediately!

www.thejoyofsoulfood.com

Seafood Creole

1/4 cup corn oil
1/4 cup flour
1 cup hot water
1 lb boneless red snapper, cut into pieces
1 lb shrimp
1 16-oz can tomato sauce
1/2 cup chopped green onion
1/4 cup chopped green bell pepper
4 cloves garlic, minced
1/4 tsp salt
1 tsp thyme
2 bay leaves
1/4 cup chopped fresh parsley
Dash cayenne pepper

1. Heat oil in a large skillet and blend in the flour. Stir constantly until flour browns. Be careful not to

scorch the roux.

2. Add the water gradually and cook until thick and smooth.

3. Add the remaining ingredients, stir well, and simmer for 15 minutes. Remove the bay leaves before serving over hot rice

www.thejoyofsoulfood.com

Seared Scallops

1 lb large bay scallops
2T Olive Oil
Kosher Salt
Pepper
Garlic

1. Rinse scallops and pat dry on paper towels

2. Heat olive oil over medium heat in medium skillet.

3. Lightly sprinkle tops of scallops with seasonings

4. Brown until golden completely and turn.

5. Scallops will turn translucent.

6. Cook for 8 minutes total

7. Eat while hot.

www.thejoyofsoulfood.com

Grilled Steak

4 T Bone or other desired tender cut of steak
4T Dale's Seasoning
1T Montreal Steak Seasoning

1. Poke steak generously with a dinner fork to tenderize.

2. Place Steaks in a Gallon Freezer Zipper Bag along with seasonings and marinade for at least an hour.

3. Spray Oven Broiling pan with cooking spray

4. Place steaks on broiler and broil at 400 degrees for 5-7 minutes on each side

or

For extra flavor, Grill outdoors after coals turn white.
Grill 5-7 minutes on each side.

www.thejoyofsoulfood.com

Fried Steak

2 T of vinegar
4 steak filets
¼ cup vegetable oil
Seasoned salt
Onion powder
Garlic powder
Black pepper
Flour

1. Heat oil in a heavy 9-10 inch skillet over medium heat.

2. Cover steaks with vinegar insuring to cover all sides.

3. Lightly sprinkle seasoned salt, onion powder, garlic powder, and black pepper.

4. Lightly flour each fillet on both sides.

5. Place seasoned and floured fillet in pan with olive oil.

6. Fry until golden brown on both sides

Succulent Roast Beef

3-4 lbs. beef brisket, eye of round or rump roast
Roasting pan
2 Tsp of butter
2 medium Carrots
1 medium chopped onion
2 stalks of celery chopped
¼ cup sliced Yellow, red, or orange pepper
Garlic powder
Seasoned salt
Rosemary
Garlic cloves
2T vinegar
1 bay leaf
Black pepper corn
1 cup of water

1. Rub seasoned salt, garlic, and black pepper all over the beef.

2. Put the beef in the roasted pan.

3. Add vinegar, garlic cloves, rosemary, black pepper corn, bay leaf, celery, carrot, onion, and 1 cup of water.

4. Pour in enough water so that the water is just touching the top of the brisket.

5. Put in the oven for about 4 hours.

www.thejoyofsoulfood.com

Fried Pork Chops

1 whole Pork Tenderloin cut into 8 crosswise pieces
1T vinegar
Seasoned Salt
Granulated Garlic
Black Pepper
1 cup flour + 1 t seasoned salt
1 cup Cooking oil

1. Over medium heat, heat canola, vegetable or peanut oil

2. Coat Pork on both sides with vinegar

3. Season chops on all sides with salt, garlic and black pepper, set aside

4. In gallon size zippered freezer bag. Shake seasoned cutlets in flour mixture.

5. Shake off excess flour

6. Fry pork chops until golden brown in hot (but not smoking) oil (3-4 minutes on each side)

7. Keep warm while cooking remaining chops.

www.thejoyofsoulfood.com

Glazed Pork Chops

4 ¾ inch Boneless Pork Chops or 8 cutlets of
Tenderloin
1T vinegar
Seasoned Salt
Granulated Garlic
Black Pepper
Cooking Spray
½ cup Apple Juice
2T Honey
1t granulated garlic

1. Coat Pork on both sides with vinegar

2. Season tenderloins on all sides with salt, garlic and black pepper, set aside

3. In a small bowl, stir together apple juice, honey and garlic

4. Spray Heavy Skillet with Cooking Spray and heat over medium heat. Skillet should have a tight fitting lid.

5. Brown pork evenly (5-6 minutes on each side)

6. Cover Pan while pork is cooking.

7. Pour apple juice mixture into pan cook uncovered for 2-3 minutes until sauce thickens slightly

www.thejoyofsoulfood.com

Baked Ham with Honey Glaze Sauce

1 ready-to-eat ham spiral sliced or not
(and whatever weight you choose)
1/4 cup whole cloves
1 can of pineapple slices
Maraschino cherries
1/4 cup dark brown sugar
1 cup honey
1/2 cup butter

1. Preheat oven to 325 degrees F
2. Be sure to remove all wrappers from ham including the hard to see wax paper.
3. Line a large baking pan with heavy aluminum foil
4. Place ham in foil lined pan.
5. Score ham, and stud with the whole cloves. Place pineapples across the top of the ham and place a maraschino cherry in the center of each pineapple.
6. In the top half of a double boiler, heat the brown sugar, honey and butter. Keep glaze warm while baking ham.
7. Brush glaze over ham, and bake ham for amount of time directed on package.
8. Baste ham every 10 to 15 minutes with the honey glaze.
9. During the last 4 to 5 minutes of baking, turn on broiler to caramelize the glaze.
10. Remove from oven, and let sit a few minutes before serving.

www.thejoyofsoulfood.com

Succulent Pork Tenderloin

1 whole Pork Tenderloin cut into 8 crosswise pieces
1T vinegar
Seasoned Salt
Granulated Garlic
Black Pepper
2T Butter

1. Coat Pork on both sides with vinegar

2. Season tenderloins on all sides with salt, garlic and black pepper, set aside

3. Over medium heat, melt butter in heavy skillet with a tight fitting lid.

4. Brown pork evenly (3-4 minutes on each side)

5. Cover Pan while pork is cooking.

6. Keep warm while cooking remaining cutlets.

www.thejoyofsoulfood.com

Dessert

Because with soul food, you must finish strong

Pecan Chocolate Chip Pound Cake

2 sticks Sweet Cream butter
1 tsp. vanilla
2 cups sugar
1 cup flake coconut
4 eggs, beaten
1 cup semi-sweet chocolate chips
2 cups flour
1 cup chopped walnuts or pecans
1 tsp. baking powder

1. 1.Cream sugar and butter.
2. 2.Add eggs one at a time beating between each egg.
3. Add rest of ingredients.
4. Bake at 350° for one hour in very large Bundt or tube pan sprayed heavily with Pam cooking spray.

Unbelievable Caramel Glaze

¾ cup sugar
½ cup water
1 stick butter
1 tsp. pure vanilla extract

5. Combine all ingredients in medium saucepan
6. boil 3 minutes on top of the stove.
7. Turn cake onto serving plate.
8. Prick cake w/ ice pick or long fork.
9. Pour glaze over hot cake.

www.thejoyofsoulfood.com

Lemon Loaf Cake

1 c. butter
1 3/4 c. sugar
5 eggs
1 tsp. vanilla
1 T lemon extract
2 c. sifted cake flour

1. Preheat oven to 325°

2. Cream butter and sugar well.

3. Add eggs, one at a time; beat well.

4. Add flavorings.

5. Add flour gradually.

6. not overbeat while adding flour but mix well.

7. Pour into lightly greased, lined 9" or 10 " inch tube pan.

8. Put cake in a cold oven and then turn oven to 325 degrees.

9. Bake for about 1 hour and 5 minutes

10. When done cake will pull away from sides of pan.

www.thejoyofsoulfood.com

Chocolate Layer Cake

1 cup butter, margarine or shortening
2 cups sugar
1 tsp salt
1 tsp vanilla
2 eggs
2 ¼ cup unsifted flour
1 cup buttermilk
½ cup cocoa
2 tsp baking soda
1 cup hot water

1. Preheat oven to 350°
2. Cream butter, sugar, salt and vanilla in large mixing bowl.
3. Add eggs, beat with mixer until mixture is very light and creamy.
4. Add flour and buttermilk; beat for 2 more minutes
5. Mix cocoa and soda in small mixing bowl; add hot water.
6. Add chocolate mixture to batter.
7. Pour into three 8" round pans and bake for 40 minutes. Frost when cooled.

Glossy Chocolate Frosting

2 cups sugar
6 T cornstarch
2 cups water
4 sq semisweet chocolate
2 T butter
1 tsp vanilla

1. Mix sugar and cornstarch in 2 qt saucepan. Add water and chocolate. Cook over medium heat until thickened. Add butter and vanilla. Stir until smooth.
2. Invert one layer of cake onto cake plate. Insert several toothpicks halfway into layer to prevent cake from shifting. Pour frosting onto layer. Add next layer and repeat process. Pour remaining frosting over top layer (without toothpicks)

www.thejoyofsoulfood.com

(Never Fail) Pineapple Upside Down Cake

Ingredients:
One box Betty Crocker yellow cake mix
2 sticks (1 cup) of sweet salted butter softened
1 can (14oz) sliced pineapples in juice
1/3 cup of water
3 large eggs
1/2 cup brown sugar
4T melted butter

1. Pour melted butter into bottom of 9x12 baking dish.
2. Crumble brown sugar over butter to coat entire bottom of pan
3. Arrange Pineapples over butter and brown sugar
5. Combine cake mix, 2 sticks softened butter, eggs, water and juice from pineapples and mix at medium speed for 2 minutes.
6. Pour cake batter over pineapples, brown sugar and butter
7. If needed use a rubber spatula to evenly spread batter.
8. Bake cake for 35 minutes in 350 degree oven until cake springs back lightly when touched. Top should be golden brown and cake should begin to pull away from the sides of pan.
9. For best presentation Flip cake onto large rectangular serving platter.

Serve with whipped cream (optional)

www.thejoyofsoulfood.com

Pound Cake with Crisp Crust

1 ½ cup butter, margarine or shortening
1 ¾ cup sugar
5 eggs
1 tsp vanilla
1 tsp lemon flavoring
2 cup flour

1. Cream shortening and sugar well. Add eggs one at a time; beat well.

2. Add flavorings

3. Add flour

4. Mix well but do not overbeat

5. Thoroughly spay 9 inch tube pan with cooking spray.

6. Pour into oiled pan

7. Bake at 325° for about 1 hour and 5 minutes or until cake tests done.

8. Cake is done when knife inserted comes out clean.

Sock it To Me Cake

Streusel Filling:
1 package Butter Recipe cake mix, divided
2 tablespoons brown sugar
2 teaspoons ground cinnamon
1 cup chopped pecans

Cake:
4 large eggs
1 cup sour cream
1/3 cup vegetable oil
1/4 cup water
1/4 cup sugar

Glaze:
1 cup powdered sugar
1 to 2 tablespoons milk

1. Preheat oven to 375°F and grease 10inch tube pan.

1. For streusel filling, Combine 2 tablespoons dry cake mix, brown sugar and cinnamon in medium bowl, stir in pecans, set aside.

2. For Cake, Combine remaining cake mix, eggs, sour cream, oil, water and sugar in large bowl.

3. Beat in medium speed with electric mixer for 2 minutes.

4. Pour 2/3 of batter into pan.

5. Sprinkle streusel filling over batter in pan.

6. Spoon remaining cake batter evenly over streusel filling.

7. Bake at 375 degrees F. for 45 to 55 minutes or until toothpick inserted in center comes out clean.

8. Cool in pan 25 minutes. Turn onto cake plate and cool completely

9. For Glaze, Combine powdered sugar and milk in small bowl. Stir until smooth and drizzle over cake.

www.thejoyofsoulfood.com

7-Up Cake

1 cup butter
1/2 cup shortening
2 cups white sugar
4 eggs
3 cups all-purpose flour
1 teaspoon vanilla extract
1 teaspoon lemon extract
7 ounces of 7-Up brand soda

1. Preheat oven to 325 °F
2. Heavily oil a 10 inch Bundt pan with cooking spray.
3. In a large bowl, cream together the butter, shortening and sugar until light and fluffy.
4. Beat in the eggs one at a time
5. stir in the vanilla and lemon extracts.
6. Beat in the flour alternately with the 7 Up soda, mixing until combined.
7. Pour batter into prepared pan.
8. Bake in the preheated oven for 70 minutes, or until a toothpick inserted into the center of the cake comes out clean.
9. Allow to cool on a cake rack for 30 minutes before removing from the pan.

www.thejoyofsoulfood.com

Caramel Layer Cake

1 cup (2 sticks) butter softened
2 cups granulated sugar
4 eggs
3 cups sifted self-rising flour
1 cup milk
1 teaspoon pure vanilla extract

1. Preheat oven to 350 degrees F. Grease and flour three 8 or 9 inch cake pans.
2. Using a mixer, cream butter until fluffy. Add granulated sugar and continue to cream well for 6 to 8 minutes.
3. Add eggs 1 at a time, beating well after each addition.
4. Add flour and milk alternately to cream mixture.
5. Add vanilla and continue to beat until just combined.
6. Divide batter equally into prepared pans.
7. Allow batter to rest in pans for about 5 minutes.
8. Bake for 25 minutes or until golden brown.

Glaze
While cake is in oven, combine butter, brown sugar, and milk in a medium saucepan,. Cook over medium heat for 3 to 5 minutes stirring constantly. Remove from heat and stir in vanilla.

Remove cake layers from oven and allow cake to remain in pans as you prepare to stack and fill. Remove first layer and turn over onto cake plate. Poke bottom of each layer of cake all over with a toothpick. Spread 1/3 of filling mixture on cake layer. Top with second layer, repeat process. Top with last layer and repeat process again. Pour glaze all over top layer.

Caramel:
2 cups (4 sticks) butter
4 cups packed dark brown sugar
1/2 cup milk
2 teaspoon pure vanilla extract
Just a dash of salt

www.thejoyofsoulfood.com

German Chocolate Cake

1 pkg Germans Sweet Chocolate
½ cup boiling water
1 cup butter, margarine or shortening
2 cups sugar
4 egg yolks, unbeaten
1 tsp vanilla
½ tsp salt
1 tsp baking soda
2 ½ cup cake flour
1 cup buttermilk
4 egg whites, stiffly beaten

1. Melt chocolate in boiling water and allow to cool.
2. Cream butter and sugar until fluffy.
3. Add egg yolks, one at a time; beat well after each
4. Add melted chocolate and vanilla and mix well
5. Sift together salt, soda and flour.
6. Add alternately with buttermilk to chocolate mixture, beat until smooth.
7. Fold in beaten egg whites.
8. Pour into three 8 or 9 inch cake layer pans, lined on bottom with wax paper.
9. Bake in 350° oven for 30 to 40 minutes. Cool.
10. Fill layers and frost top and sides with cocoanut pecan frostings.

Coconut Pecan Frosting

1 cup evaporated milk
1 cup sugar
3 egg yolks
¼ lb butter
1 tsp vanilla
1 1/3 cup coconut
1 cup chopped pecans

Combine milk, sugar, egg yolks and butter; add vanilla. Cook over low heat, stirring constantly until thickened, about 12 minutes. Add coconut and pecans. Beat until thick.

www.thejoyofsoulfood.com

Carrot Cake with Cream Cheese Frosting

3 cups flour
2 tsp baking soda
3 tsp cinnamon
½ tsp salt
1 ½ cups vegetable oil
2 cups sugar
2 cups grated carrots
½ cup chopped walnuts (optional)
2 tsp vanilla
3 eggs

1. Sift together flour, soda, cinnamon, and salt.
2. Mix together oil and sugar in separate bowl.
3. Add half the dry ingredients, mix well. Beat in carrots, and nuts.
4. Add vanilla and remaining dry ingredients. Add eggs one at a time, beating until well blended after each addition.
5. Pour into greased 9 x 12 inch pan.
6. Bake at 350° until golden brown and cake tests done.

Cream Cheese Icing:
½ stick butter (softened)
1 box powdered sugar
1 - 8 oz box creamed cheese
½ tsp lemon extract
1 tsp pure vanilla extract

Blend all ingredients together and frost top of cake.

Coconut Cake

½ lb butter
2 cups sugar
4 eggs separated
2 2/3 cup cake flour
4 tsp baking powder
Pinch of salt
1 cup milk
1 tsp vanilla

1. Heavily spray 3 8 or 9 inch cake pans with cooking spray.
2. Preheat oven to 375 °
3. Cream butter and sugar well.
4. Add egg yolks one at a time, mix well.
5. Sift flour, baking powder, and salt together.
6. Add alternately with milk. Add vanilla.
7. Beat egg whites until stiff, fold into mixture.
8. Bake at 375 ° for 20-25 minutes.

Coconut Filling
1 egg yolk
1 cup milk
1 cup sugar
1 T cornstarch
1 tsp vanilla
1 cup grated coconut

1. Mix together all ingredients except coconut.
2. Cook in double boiler over low heat until thickened.
3. Cool
4. Add coconut to cooled frosting mixture and ice cake.

www.thejoyofsoulfood.com

Red Velvet Cake

2 cups sugar
1/2 pound (2 sticks) butter, at room temperature
2 eggs
3 tablespoons cocoa powder
2 ounces red food coloring
2 1/2 cups cake flour
1 teaspoon salt
1 cup buttermilk
1 teaspoon vanilla extract
1/2 teaspoon baking soda
1 tablespoon vinegar

Frosting

1 (8-ounce) package cream cheese
1 stick butter, softened
1 (1-pound) box confectioners' sugar
1 cup pecan halves
2 T milk

1. Preheat oven to 350 degrees
2. In a mixing bowl, cream the sugar and butter, beat until light and fluffy.
3. Add the eggs one at a time and mix well after each addition.
4. Mix cocoa and food coloring together and then add to sugar mixture; mix well.
5. Sift together flour and salt. Add flour mixture to the creamed mixture alternately with buttermilk. Blend in vanilla.
6. In a small bowl, combine baking soda and vinegar and add to mixture.
7. Pour batter into 3 (8-inch) round greased and floured pans. Bake for 20 to 25 minutes, or until a toothpick inserted into the center comes out clean.
8. Remove from heat and cool completely before frosting.

Frosting

Blend cream cheese and butter together in a mixing bowl. Add sugar and milk and blend. Spread icing between layers and on top and sides of cooled cake. Decorate top of cake with pecan halves.

www.thejoyofsoulfood.com

Strawberry Shortcake

2 cups Real whipped cream
3 T of sugar
1 pint of Sliced strawberries
2 boxes of yellow cake mix
Butter (optional)
Pure vanilla extract (optional)

1. Prepare cake as directed on package and allow to cool completely. (You may substitute butter for vegetable oil and add 1 tsp of pure vanilla extract for richer texture and flavor.)
2. Remove stems from strawberries and slide thinly.
3. In a large bowl combine 2 cups whipping cream with 3 T of sugar and blend on high until soft peaks form.
4. Once cake has cooled completely, spread the lower layer of the cake with the whipped cream icing. Add a layer of sliced strawberries evenly.
5. You may add toothpicks to prevent top layer from sliding. Insert toothpicks halfway into bottom layer and gently place inverted top layer over bottom layer.
6. Add whipped cream to top layer of cake
7. Decoratively Garnish with strawberries .
8. Serve with an extra dollop of whipped cream.

Berry Cobbler

Filling
2 cups blueberries, raspberries or sliced strawberries (any combination)
1 cup of sugar
1 tsp vanilla

Batter
1 stick of butter
1 ¼ flour
¾ cup sugar
1 cup milk

1. Heat oven to 350 degrees
2. Combine 2 cups of sliced strawberry, raspberries or blueberries or any combination and 1 cup of sugar [depending on your sweet tooth]

3. Let it sit for 20 minutes or heat partially to dissolve sugar.

4. Melt one stick of butter in a 1-1/2 quart baking dish.

5. Stir together 11/4 cup self-rising flour and ¾ cup of sugar.

6. Stir in one cup of milk until most of the lumps disappear.

7. Pour into baking dish of melted butter.

8. Gently layer berries on top.

9. Do NOT Stir.

10. Bake for 45 minutes at 350 degrees.

www.thejoyofsoulfood.com

Peach Cobbler

1 stick butter
1 cup of sugar
1 can of peaches
1 box of cook and serve vanilla pudding (Don't use instant pudding)
1 t of vanilla extract
1/2 tsp cinnamon
2 pre made pie crusts

1. Preheat oven to 425 degrees
2. Add butter to a cold saucepan and turn heat to medium.
3. Add sugar, peaches, pudding, vanilla extract, and cinnamon.
4. Stir until all butter is melted and sugar and pudding are dissolved.
5. Lay pre-made pie crust in the pie pan stretching into corners and completely up the sides of the pan.
6. Pour hot peach mixture into the pie crust.
7. Add second pie crust to cover top of peach mixture. Crimp edges together
8. Make several (5-7)vents in the top of the pie crust.
9. Brush the top of the pie crust and ridges with melted butter.
10. Sprinkle granulated sugar on the top of the pie crust.

11. Bake for 30 minutes.
12. Serve hot with ice cream

www.thejoyofsoulfood.com

Southern Pecan Pie

1/4 cup butter or margarine
2/3 cup firmly packed brown sugar
Dash of salt
3/4 cup dark corn syrup
3 eggs, well beaten
1 cup pecan halves
1 tsp vanilla extract
8-inch unbaked pie shell

1. Cream together butter or margarine, brown sugar and salt; stir in remaining ingredients.

2. Pour into unbaked pie shell.

3. Bake in very hot oven (450 degrees F.) for 10 minutes; then reduce heat to moderate (350 degrees F.)and bake 30 to 35 minutes longer, or until knife inserted comes out clean.

4. Cool and serve with whipped cream or ice cream, if desired.

Apple Pie

2 Pastry for 9 inch pie crust
2/3 cups sugar
¼ cup all purpose flour
½ tsp nutmeg
½ tsp cinnamon
Dash of salt
8 thinly sliced medium apples
1 tsp lemon juice
3 T butter

1. Heat oven to 425°.
2. Place one pastry shell in bottom of oiled pie plate.
3. In a large mixing bowl, combine sugar, flour, nutmeg, cinnamon and salt.
4. Stir in apples and lemon juice and allow to sit for 5 minutes
5. Pour apple mixture into prepared pastry shell.
6. Dot apple mixture with butter
7. Cover with top pastry crusts.
8. Cut one inch slits into top of pastry crust.
9. Seal and flute crust.
10. Brush top with melted butter and sprinkle lightly with granulated sugar.
11. Bake 40-50 minutes or until crust is golden brown and juice bubbles through slits.

www.thejoyofsoulfood.com

Sweet Potato Pie

3 large cooked sweet potatoes, peeled and mashed
3/4 cup sugar
1/2 cup egg substitute
2 tsp vanilla
1 tsp lemon-flavored extract
1 Tbsp butter-flavored extract
1 tsp cinnamon
1 tsp nutmeg
1 tsp lemon juice
1 1/2 cups fat-free (skim) evaporated milk
1 9-inch pie shell

1. Heat the oven to 350 F.
2. Mix all the ingredients together and beat until smooth. Pour into the pie shell and bake for 40 minutes
3. Allow to cool and serve with whip cream or ice cream

Chocolate Chip Cookies

1 cup butter or margarine, softened

1 cup white sugar

1 cup packed brown sugar

2 eggs

2 teaspoons vanilla extract

3 cups all-purpose flour

1 teaspoon baking soda

2 teaspoons hot water

1/2 teaspoon salt

2 cups semisweet chocolate chips

1 1/4 cup chopped walnuts

1. Preheat oven to 350 degrees F
2. Cream together the butter, white sugar, and brown sugar until smooth. Beat in the eggs one at a time, then stir in the vanilla. Dissolve baking soda in hot water. Add to batter along with salt. Stir in flour, chocolate chips, and nuts. Drop by large spoonfuls onto ungreased pans.
3. Bake for about 10 minutes in the preheated oven, or until edges are nicely browned.

Oatmeal Cookies

1 cup butter, softened
1 cup white sugar
1 cup packed brown sugar
2 eggs
1 teaspoon vanilla extract
2 cups all-purpose flour
1 teaspoon baking soda
1 teaspoon salt
1 teaspoons ground cinnamon
3 cups quick cooking oats

1. In a medium bowl, cream together butter, white sugar, and brown sugar. Beat in eggs one at a time, then stir in vanilla. Combine flour, baking soda, salt, and cinnamon; stir into the creamed mixture. Mix in oats. Cover, and chill dough for at least one hour.
2. Preheat the oven to 375 degrees F (190 degrees C). Grease cookie sheets. Roll the dough into 2 inch balls, and place 2 inches apart on cookie sheets. Flatten each cookie with a fork.
3. Bake for 8 to 10 minutes in preheated oven. Allow cookies to cool on baking sheet for 5 minutes before transferring to a wire rack to cool completely.

www.thejoyofsoulfood.com

Snickerdoodles

1 cup shortening or margarine
(butter makes cookie crunchy)
1 ½ c sugar
2 eggs
2 ¾ c sifted flour
2 tsp cream of tartar
1 tsp baking soda
¼ tsp salt

1. Mix shortening, sugar, and eggs thoroughly. Sift flour, cream of tartar, baking soda, and salt together.

2. Stir into sugar mixture.

3. Roll dough into 2" balls

4. Roll balls in topping mixture to cover completely

5. Place about 2 inches apart on baking sheet.

6. Bake at 400° for 8-10 minutes.

Topping Mixture:
2 T sugar
2tsp cinnamon
Combine and Mix well in separate plate

www.thejoyofsoulfood.com

Peanut Butter Cookies

1 cup unsalted butter
1 cup smooth peanut butter
1 cup white sugar
1 cup firmly packed brown sugar
2 eggs
2 1/2 cups all-purpose flour
1 teaspoon baking powder
1/2 teaspoon salt
1 1/2 teaspoons baking soda

1. Preheat oven to 375°
2. Cream together butter, peanut butter and sugars. Beat in eggs.
3. In a separate bowl, sift together flour, baking powder, baking soda, and salt. Stir into batter. Put batter in refrigerator for 1 hour.
4. Roll into 1 inch balls and put on baking sheets. Flatten each ball with a fork, dipped in sugar, making a criss-cross pattern.
5. Bake in a preheated 375 degrees F oven for about 10 minutes or until cookies begin to brown. Do not over-bake.

Lemon Cookies

1 (18.25 ounce) package lemon cake mix
2 eggs
1/3 cup vegetable oil
2 teaspoon lemon juice
1/3 cup confectioners' sugar for decoration

1. Preheat oven to 375 degrees F (190 degrees C).
2. Pour cake mix into a large bowl. Stir in eggs, oil, and lemon juice until well blended.
3. Drop teaspoonfuls of dough into a bowl of confectioners' sugar. Roll them around until they're lightly covered.
4. Place balls on ungreased cookie sheet 2 inches apart.
5. Bake for 6 to 9 minutes in the preheated oven.
6. The bottoms will be light brown, and the insides chewy.

www.thejoyofsoulfood.com

Beverages
Hot and Cold and always sweet

SHAM-pagne

great for weddings (or white carpet)
1 qt apple juice
2 large bottles of ginger ale
Strawberries for garnish

Combine chilled Juice and chilled Ginger ale. Add one strawberry to each wine flute and pour chilled SHAM-pagne to fill the glass. Cheers!

Watermelon Punch

Fruit from one whole large Seedless Watermelon
1 large can frozen lime concentrate
1 cup sugar
2 cups of water
2 cups of ice

Puree watermelon in batches in the blender and pour into punch bowl.
Blend lime concentrate, sugar, water and ice.
Add lime mixture to watermelon mixture

Serve over ice.

www.thejoyofsoulfood.com

Frappe

(Birthday party punch)
1 gallon of sherbet-any flavor is fine
2 -2liter bottles of sprite, 7Up or Ginger ale

Put sherbet in large punch bowl
Pour carbonated beverage over sherbet and allow to melt
Serve with ladle into cups as sherbet dissolves.

Sherbet Punch

2 large cans of pineapple juice
1 qt sherbet
1 qt vanilla ice cream
2 liters of ginger ale

Combine juice sherbet and ice cream in a large bowl and blend.
Add ginger ale and serve immediately.

Cranberry Fruit Punch

3 pt cranberry juice cocktail
3 cup orange juice
¾ cup lemon juice
1 ½ cup pineapple juice
1 ½ cup sugar
3 cups water

Combine all ingredients. Stir until sugar dissolves. Add 1 cup fresh whole
cranberries for garnish. Serve over ice.

Tropical Fruit Smoothie

12 oz fresh strawberries, stems removed
2 ripe bananas
1 can mango nectar or 2 ripe mangos
4 tablespoons turbinado (raw) sugar or honey
1 cup ice cubes
3/4 cup milk or yogurt

Wash strawberries and remove banana and mango peels. Combine all ingredients in a blender, and process until smooth.

www.thejoyofsoulfood.com

Bridal Punch

2 ½ cups of water
3 cups sugar
3 cups pineapple juice
5 cups orange juice
1 cup lemon juice
3 cups cold water
2 liters of ginger ale
1 cup of strawberries whole with stem removed.
Combine all ingredients and blend until sugar is dissolved.

Spiced Tea

1 gallon water
3 sticks cinnamon
3 tsp whole cloves
3 cups sugar
9 tea bags
2 cups orange juice
1/3 cup lemon juice

Boil water with cinnamon, cloves, and sugar for 5 minutes. Add tea. Turn off heat and steep for 5 minutes. Strain, add juices. Serve hot or cold over ice.

Hot Apple Cider

1 qt apple juice or apple cider
2 cinnamon sticks
1 tsp ginger
1tsp allspice
5 whole cloves
1 cup sugar
1 cup orange juice
Combine all ingredients in saucepan over medium heat.
Stir until sugar dissolves and heat until it simmers.
Allow cider to simmer for 10 minutes.
Serve while hot into mugs, do not serve spices.

Homemade Hot Cocoa

4 cups milk
1/3 cup cocoa powder
1 cup sugar
Dash salt

Combine all ingredients in small saucepan and stir until
cocoa dissolves
Heat thoroughly but do not allow to boil.
Serve hot with marshmallows or candy canes as garnish.

www.thejoyofsoulfood.com

Eggnog

4 eggs separated
Sugar
¼ tsp salt
1 1/3 cup mashed banana
2 tsp vanilla
3 cups milk
1 cup half and half
¼ tsp nutmeg
¼ cup light rum

1. Beat eggnog, 2 T sugar and salt in large mixing bowl until light. Beat in mashed bananas, vanilla, milk, half and half and nutmeg. Stir in rum, and chill.

2. Beat egg whites in small bowl until soft peaks form.

3. Gradually beat in 1/3 cup sugar until stiff peaks form.

4. Fold egg whites into banana mixture. Refrigerate until ready to serve.

5. Sprinkle with additional nutmeg.

6. Yields 12 servings.

www.thejoyofsoulfood.com

Lemonade

2 cups sugar
8 cups water
1 1/2 cups lemon juice

1. In a saucepan, combine sugar and 1 cup water. Bring to boil and stir until sugar is dissolved. Allow to cool to room temperature, then cover and refrigerate until chilled.
2. Stir together chilled syrup, lemon juice and remaining 7 cups water.

Strawberry Lemonade

1 pitcher of lemonade prepared as above
1 pint of strawberries with stems removed
3T grenadine

1. Blend strawberries with 2 cups water.
2. Pour pureed strawberry mixture and grenadine into pitcher of lemonade and stir.
3. Serve over ice.

Perfect Georgia Sweet Tea

2 cups boiling water
6 tea bags
3/4 cup white sugar
6 cups cool water

1. Sprinkle a pinch of baking soda into a 64-ounce, heat-proof, glass pitcher. Pour in boiling water, and add tea bags. Cover, and allow to steep for 15 minutes.

2. Remove tea bags, and discard; stir in sugar until dissolved. Pour in cool water, then refrigerate until cold.

www.thejoyofsoulfood.com

Dear Friends,

Thank you for joining me on my journey to enjoy all the best of soul food while maintaining healthier eating habits.

I hope you have enjoyed the recipes here. I hope something reminded you of fun times at your grandmothers or that you were able to put a smile on your spouse's face with your new found culinary prowess. Most of all, I hope you feel like a real cook because you are! It's as simple as following these easy step by step instructions.

I want to hear from you. Please write and tell me about your experiences with the recipes. Please visit me at www.thejoyofsoulfood.com and leave your comments.

The code for video demonstrations is: soulfoodislove. Look for holiday specific cookbooks in the future.

God Bless You!

Love,
Pamela Holmes

Made in the USA
Columbia, SC
22 January 2025

52238416R00070